sundance
**LITTLE GREEN
READERS**

Recycling

Focus: Recycling

Meredith Costain

Recycling means using old things again. All of these things can be used again.

We can recycle old cans.
Old cans can be made
into new cans.

We can recycle old paper.
Old paper can be made
into new paper.

We can recycle old tires.
Old tires can be made
into rubber mats.

We can recycle old wood.
Old wood can be made
into a table.

We can recycle old glass
bottles.
Old glass bottles can be
made into glass jars.

Old plastic bottles can be made into new plastic chairs. Recycling means making new things from old things.